POCKETBOOKS
by BroadStreet

2-MINUTE DEVOTIONS FOR *Women*

BroadStreet
PUBLISHING

BroadStreet Publishing Group, LLC.
Savage, Minnesota, USA
Broadstreetpublishing.com

2-Minute Devotions for Women

9781424568482
9781424568499 eBook

Typesetting and design by Garborg Design Works | garborgdesign.com
Compiled and edited by Michelle Winger | literallyprecise.com

Printed in China.

25 26 27 28 29 30 31 7 6 5 4 3 2 1

Even in your darkest hours, you can know true joy because God is your guardian.

INTRODUCTION

Life has become increasingly busy. We jump from one responsibility to the next with little time to breathe in between. We settle for things that satisfy our immediate needs, but we long for more.

2-Minute Devotions for Women presents 100 quick meditations for you to reflect on. A moment spent in God's presence empowers you to be a woman of strength, dignity, and grace. Be inspired and refreshed as you take a break to ponder each Scripture, devotion, and prayer.

Enjoy this lifegiving interruption that provides satisfaction beyond your temporary needs and desires, peace that lightens the load of your responsibilities, and love that helps you share God's goodness with the people around you.

DAY 1

REST SECURE

I keep my eyes always on the LORD.
With him at my right hand, I will not be shaken.
Therefore my heart is glad and my tongue rejoices;
my body also will rest secure.

PSALM 16:8-9 NIV

No matter where you are, God is there also. While there may be times when we ache to hide from him in our shame, he is a constant presence. The beautiful thing about his omnipresence is that we have a steady and consistent companion who is always ready to help in times of trouble.

We have no reason to fear the things that the world may throw our way. We've got the best protector of all at our side! Are you asking for his help in times of worry and woe, or are you turning inward to try to solve your problems? Let God be your refuge. Nothing is too big or too small for him. Even in your darkest hours, you can know true joy because he is your guardian.

God, I cast my cares and distress on you. Thank you that you can handle them, and I don't have to.

DAY 2

SET APART

"Before you were born I set you apart."

JEREMIAH 1:5 NIV

Nobody was an accident or an afterthought. The Lord has carefully crafted every person uniquely. He loved each of us before we were even born because he planned in his heart and mind exactly how we were meant to be.

Sometimes we try to deviate away from how the Lord created us and the calling he has placed on our lives, but as we search for peace to accept who we are and how we were formed, we can have confidence that the Lord truly knows us. He knew us before the world began to hurt and influence us, and he knows how to restore us as well.

Thank you, Father, for setting me apart. You know me perfectly because you made me.

DAY 3

Different Gifts

In his grace, God has given us different gifts for doing certain things well. So if God has given you the ability to prophesy, speak out with as much faith as God has given you.

ROMANS 12:6 NLT

Of what benefit is it if someone were to give a child a gift, but that child never opened it or used it? God has given each of us natural abilities, talents, and spiritual gifts. He wants to teach us how to use them and what they are for. With the faith that we have, he asks us to step out in our gifts. In time our faith will grow.

Imagine if the child who received the gift only wanted to play by himself. God's great plans for giving gifts includes serving and encouraging the entire body of believers. He has given each of us a special position in his family and the tools we need to play our part well. Our gifts are not for us alone but should be used to help others.

God, give me the faith I need to step out and use my gifts. I know you have placed them there for me to bless others.

DAY 4

Chosen Ones

You are a chosen race, a royal priesthood, a holy nation, a people for his possession, so that you may proclaim the praises of the one who called you out of darkness into his marvelous light.

1 Peter 2:9 CSB

On occasion, we need a little nudge for all the pieces of our disposition to fall into alignment with God's. Today's nudge is a grand reminder of our identity as a Christian body. We are each holy priests serving the Living God! He is risen, and we are singly and corporately his. Because of this, we each walk in his light, and we shepherd others into the light as well.

Sometimes, it is difficult to get rid of the grumpy feelings of the day. It seems okay to have a lower opinion of ourselves and our circumstances (and maybe other people). But the truth is that God's opinion is our opinion, and we are to shout that in everything we do. Priests carry a message to the people. What message are you carrying today?

God, help me to carry the message of your good news everywhere I go. I want to be ready to share your love with everyone I meet.

God loved you before you were born; he planned exactly how you were meant to be.

DAY 5

A Genuine Love

Love each other with genuine affection and take delight in honoring each other.

Romans 12:10 NLT

One of the most difficult things to do is to love someone who doesn't want to be loved. To love those who push you away every time you try to help, those who are difficult, and those who are maybe even a little mean is discouraging, defeating, even costly.

Genuine love keeps showing up. It continues to extend a hand of grace. It serves in every capacity possible. It sees the whole person. Sometimes the hardness of a person is just a mask. Often those difficult people need to know deep down inside that they are worth the effort.

God, there are people in my life who are difficult to love. Help me to reach out to them and let them know that they are seen and loved by you.

DAY 6

WRITTEN

A person may have many ideas
concerning God's plan for his life,
but only the designs of his purpose
will succeed in the end.
PROVERBS 19:21 TPT

Our futures, just like our pasts, are in the hands of God. We were not an afterthought or a disposable extra detail. In fact, we were created for a very specific part in God's family, and we are irreplaceable in the eyes of the Lord. He made each of us from the outpouring of his love, and by his design we came to be.

During the hard days we can remember that the Lord has a purpose for those as well. Every one of our days are known by God and destined for us even before our lives began. The point of the hard days is not to just move us to the good days. There are incredible lessons to be learned and insights to be gleaned from every day we are given.

Father, help me to have joy and appreciation during the difficult times in my life. There is always something good to be learned from you.

DAY 7

Busyness

"Come away by yourselves to a secluded place and rest a while." (For there were many people coming and going, and they did not even have time to eat.)

Mark 6:31 NASB

Our lives are so full that we often have difficulty finding time to spend with Jesus. We have so much that demands our attention, it can be hard to find time to consecrate a portion of our day to God. He, who has existed for eternity, is not bound by time. Because he is outside of time, time does not limit him the way that it limits us. When we take even a few sacred minutes to spend in his presence in the midst of our busy day, he can meet us there and download deep truths to our hearts.

In the days when you feel you don't even have time to eat, ask God to give you the grace to find a few moments to slip away alone in his presence. God will speak volumes to a heart that is open to his truth—even over the hustle and bustle of your busiest days.

God, I open my heart to your truth. I want your Word to be my guide even in the busy moments.

DAY 8

HEART TRUTH

O LORD, who shall sojourn in your tent?
He who speaks the truth in his heart.

PSALM 15:1-2 ESV

Our thoughts need coaching because most of the time they will derail. It is natural to become self-focused throughout the day. In doing so, insecurities and fears can subconsciously be strengthened. It's important to pause throughout the day and take stock in what we have given our minds to.

There is great value in actively controlling your mind. It is critical to speak the truth to our hearts. Don't be discouraged when you see that you aren't walking closely with God. View it as a revelation from God to help you correct your course.

God, I need your strength to align my mind with your truth. Thank you that you are happy to give that to me.

Your gifts are not for you alone but should be used to help others.

DAY 9

WALK WISELY

Be very careful, then, how you live—not as unwise but as wise, making the most of every opportunity, because the days are evil.

EPHESIANS 5:15-16 NIV

Paul had been beaten, shipwrecked, stoned, imprisoned, and homeless. He was well aware that any day could be his last. Although we may not have been beckoned by death as often as he, we also do not know when our lives will end.

Our time on earth is not just short, it is filled with evil days as well. Everywhere we look, unwise people live for themselves and reject the grace of God. Our lives should be led by the wisdom that comes from God so we can be pleasing to him and an example to others. When we live like this, we can make the most of every opportunity to witness to others.

God, help me to walk in wisdom and not foolishness. I want to make the most of every opportunity you give me.

DAY 10

Accept Your Gift

Do not neglect the gift that is in you, which was given to you by prophecy with the laying on of the hands of the eldership. Meditate on these things; give yourself entirely to them, that your progress may be evident to all.

1 Timothy 4:14-15 NKJV

Paul wrote to Timothy, encouraging him to use his gift of teaching. Of what profit is it to simply possess gifts if we forgo using them? God has invested a unique set of traits in each of us to reflect himself and to play an intrinsic part in his plan.

God will teach us how to use our gifts and offer us opportunities to put them to use if we trust his leading and guiding. It is important that we refrain from becoming jealous of someone else's gift and praise God for the gifts he has given to us, learning to use them for his glory.

God, show me how I can use my gifts for your glory and to bless those around me.

DAY 11

POVERTY

One who is gracious to a poor man lends to the LORD, and He will repay him for his good deed.

PROVERBS 19:17 NASB

People can be poor in many ways. In our environment, we may not come across true poverty or see homeless people in our day-to-day lives. But there are those who suffer from poverty of joy, hope, and love. There are those around you, even today, who are hurting from their lack of being loved by someone or suffering from despair.

Ask the Holy Spirit to show you those who are poor in spirit and find a way to bring grace into their situation. It might be practical help, a kind word, or an invitation out for coffee. Let the grace that dwells in you be poured out on those around you and know that your heavenly Father will be overjoyed that you are sharing his love.

God, I have seen poverty in the people around me. Show me how I can lend to the poor.

DAY 12

FLOODWATERS

The LORD rules over the floodwaters.
The LORD reigns as king forever.

PSALM 29:10 NLT

Picture a season in your life where you were knee-deep in busyness, swallowed in sadness, or buried in exhaustion. Picture that season and how you looked, acted, reacted, and survived.

Now picture the King of the heavens and earth. See how he rules over the entire earth. This powerful God wants you to lean on him, and that seems easy to do when you understand just how great and mighty he is. If you have woken up feeling tired, lean on the strength of your Savior.

Father, sometimes I feel weary and weak. I rely on you in those moments to be my source of power.

Genuine love keeps showing up.

DAY 13

Cheerful Face

A joyful heart makes a cheerful face,
But when the heart is sad, the spirit is broken.
Proverbs 15:13 NASB

Real joy is lasting and is not deterred by circumstances here on earth, for it is caused by the hope we have in Jesus for our eternity. Since it is secured in that which will not fail, it cannot be broken by anything we know to be momentary. Our joy is a gift that cannot be taken away. It helps us to find cheer when everything in our lives seems to be in disarray.

There will be times of sadness in all our lives. Each one of us will face our own tragedies. It is when we give way to sadness and allow it to dictate our condition that our spirit is broken and we can no longer find the motivation to press forward.

God, with eternity in my heart, I will cling to the joy you have given me. That will give me the determination I need to overcome.

DAY 14

Slaying the Giants

David said to the Philistine, "You come against me with sword and spear and javelin, but I come against you in the name of the LORD Almighty, the God of the armies of Israel, whom you have defied. This day the LORD will deliver you into my hands."

1 Samuel 17:45-46 NIV

Goliath had been taunting the Israelites for forty days, daring someone to come fight him. Goliath was huge and terrifying, and nobody was brave enough to fight him except that shepherd boy who gathered five smooth stones from the stream.

We all have giants in our lives. Maybe not one named Goliath, but giants of fear and stress. Our giants are real and they can rock our world, stressing us to the limit. In those moments, we need to remember what that shepherd boy did: he wasn't going out to fight Goliath under his own strength; he was going to face the giant armed with God. That's where our power lies. The next time you're weighed down with stress over situations that you can't fix, go to the one who can.

God, help me to take my eyes off the giants and fix them on you. You can help me.

DAY 15

ASSEMBLING TOGETHER

Let us consider how to stimulate one another to love and good deeds, not forsaking our own assembling together, as is the habit of some.

HEBREWS 10:24 NASB

All throughout Scripture, God's intention for us to live as a community of believers is revealed. He created us to need each other so we could learn how to put others first and lay ourselves down. Here, we are reminded to encourage others toward love and good works.

We have a biblical responsibility to fellowship with others so that we can continue to learn and grow through relationships, and so we can help bear their burdens and encourage them. Relationships can be the most difficult element in life to navigate. Rather than moving on when they become strained or require maintenance, fight for love and unity with God's strength.

God, when it becomes difficult to be around someone, help me to humble myself and attempt to amend the relationship.

DAY 16

Feeling Small

"The Son of Man came to seek and to save the lost."

Luke 19:10 NIV

When our bodies are tired and our spirits match, it is easy to look at the great big world and feel very small. We try not to pay attention to numbers, but we do. We see how few likes we get on social media or watch promotions fly by to land on others. We wonder why we are spinning our wheels. Why are the big bucks heading in another direction? And sometimes it hits us.

I'm just a small person.

Small people have great value to Jesus. Sooner or later all of us look at the world and compare. The scope of our tiny place in a big world makes us feel insignificant, and we head to bed wondering if all the hard work has any worth. Jesus came for all. He is our salvation and significance. Little people with a great God have a divine purpose. Think about that today.

God, thank you for the purpose and significance you have given me.

God will speak volumes to a heart that is open to his truth.

DAY 17

Refuge and Strength

God is our refuge and strength,
always ready to help in times of trouble.
So we will not fear when earthquakes come
and the mountains crumble into the sea.

Psalm 46:1-2 NLT

Since we have an eternal perspective and we know that God is our help in times of trouble, we can have confidence rather than fear when disaster strikes. When others are overcome with worry or doubt, we continue to focus on God and trust his hand will guide us.

Our strength and our courage come from God. Even if everything is crumbling down around us, we can find refuge in him because he is greater than the world. He is always prepared to offer his people comfort and hope. We do not need to worry about the future like those who rely on themselves. We don't seek shelter behind temporary shields because God is our covering. We don't cower in the face of danger like those whose only defense is themselves.

God, you are my refuge and my strength. Help me to remember that in every moment.

DAY 18

SLEEP LIKE A KING

That night the king could not sleep; so he ordered the book of the chronicles, the record of his reign, to be brought in and read to him.

ESTHER 6:1 NIV

Some nights we collapse into bed. Other nights it's a long process of winding down and letting the day's busyness melt away. You may have a bedtime routine which helps you relax—a book, a hot bath, or a nice cup of chamomile tea. Most would not choose King Xerxes' strategy; however, the sheer boredom of reading records would likely put anyone to sleep.

God uses even sleepless nights for his purposes. Can it be God has your eyes open and mind alert for an unseen reason? Your reason may be as simple as prayer. Perhaps someone needs intercession or encouragement. God used the king's sleepless night to express gratitude for a past blessing. But ultimately his insomnia humiliated God's enemies and saved a nation. There is always a greater plan at work.

God, when I wake up in the night, please bring to mind who I could pray for.

DAY 19

VULNERABILITY

He gives us more grace. That is why Scripture says:
"God opposes the proud
but shows favor to the humble."
JAMES 4:6 NIV

Some of the most substantial and ultimately wonderful changes in our lives come from moments of vulnerability: laying our cards on the table, so to speak. But vulnerability takes one key ingredient: humility. And humility is not easy. Isn't it easier to pretend conflict never happened than to face the fact that we made a mistake and wronged another person? It's not always easy to humble ourselves and fight for the resolution in an argument—especially when it means admitting our failures.

Who are you in the face of conflict? Do you avoid apologizing in an attempt to save face? Does your pride get in the way of vulnerability, or are you willing and ready to humble yourself for restoration in your relationships? God says that he will give favor and wisdom to the humble.

God, please show me how I need to humble myself for the sake of a restored relationship.

DAY 20

FAITH OR SIGHT

We are always confident and know that as long as we are at home in the body we are away from the Lord. For we live by faith, not by sight.

2 CORINTHIANS 5:6-7 NIV

Sometimes we demand a lot of God. "God, I'd like this house," "God, this is my dream job," "I'm so ready to have a husband," and we wait in expectation. We wait for him to do the impossible. We wait for him to give us the desires of our hearts. Because if he does, then he is most definitely all-powerful. If he does, he heard your cry and answered. If he does, he loves you. This is living by sight.

In 2 Corinthians it says we live by faith, not sight. We often doubt God. Living by faith is giving up any control we thought we had, and sitting in the passenger seat in eager anticipation of where God is taking us.

Father, today I let go of unfulfilled desires and start living by faith. Thank you that you want what is best for me.

God's joy is a gift that cannot be taken away.

DAY 21

UNEXPECTED ANGELS

The LORD hears good people when they cry out to him, and he saves them from all their troubles.

PSALM 34:17 NCV

Sometimes your rescue can come in the form of another person. We cry out to God and ask him for help, but we shouldn't presume to know exactly how he is going to help us. God has humanity in his image and can express himself through people with their kind acts, words of encouragement, and often a great piece of advice or wisdom.

Thank God today for the people that he has put in your life and the unexpected ways that he can use them to encourage you. Thank him for revealing himself to you through others. Thank him that you can be part of the healing and grace he longs to share with the broken world.

God, thank you that you work through your people in unexpected ways. I choose to believe that for myself today.

DAY 22

SHOWERS OF BLESSINGS

"I will strengthen you, I will help you,
I will uphold you with my righteous right hand."
ISAIAH 41:10 ESV

Jill's newborn son, Adam, was beautiful. But as the months went by, he started missing milestones that babies are supposed to reach at various ages. It soon became clear Adam would never talk, sit up, or walk. More children joined their family. Jill loved them all, with a tender love for the little son who required extra care. She didn't begrudge a minute of all the care she gave, but she was beyond exhausted.

Many women would have folded under all the stress and physical demands. But not Jill. She had discovered the best place to get the strength she needed. She didn't have time to sit down to read, so she played an audio Bible, the promises from God's Word soaking into her weary soul. She prayed as she folded laundry. And she played worship music. The precious words of the songs showered her with blessings of God's power and comfort.

God, thank you that even when I have heavy burdens, I can discover your showers of blessing.

DAY 23

TEARS ON MY PILLOW

Weeping may tarry for the night,
but joy comes with the morning.

PSALM 30:5 ESV

Still half-asleep, Rose reached over in the darkness to put her arm around her husband... and felt nothing. She jerked awake, raw grief overwhelming her as tears soaked into her pillowcase. He wasn't there anymore. He never would be again. Rose knew Rob was with Jesus now, that he was in a better place, but that didn't lessen the pain of her sweetheart being gone.

Perhaps you're like Rose. You've lost someone close to you. Perhaps your grief is so deep that it's hard to catch your breath. You wonder if you'll ever smile again or how you'll make it through the weeks and months ahead. But you will. Cling to Jesus. Life will be different, but the sun will shine again. God will not leave you alone, and he will be enough for all that you're going through.

God, you are my joy in the morning. Thank you for not leaving me alone in my grief.

DAY 24

HEALTHY TREES

Like trees planted in the Temple of the LORD, they will grow strong in the courtyards of our God.

PSALM 92:13 NCV

Take a moment to reflect on a time when you felt you were giving the best of yourself. You may be thinking of times when you were utilizing your gifts and talents and could witness your positive influence in others around you. You may not have to reflect back far, or you could be wondering where those times have gone!

Jesus describes himself as the vine. If we are being nourished from that source, we will produce fruit. In the times where we feel like we are not flourishing, it may be that the Father needs to do some necessary pruning—for the health of both the branch and the whole vine.

Thank you, Father, for the pruning that brings fruit into my life.

When you are weighed down with situations that you can't fix, go to the one who can.

DAY 25

APPROACH GOD

In him and through faith in him we may approach God with freedom and confidence.

EPHESIANS 3:12 NIV

The access we have to approach God in prayer comes from Christ's sacrifice for our sins. We have been made pure and clean, so we can freely approach him. The confidence we have to come before him is because of our faith in Christ's sacrifice for us. He died for us, purified us, established our faith, and invited us to approach God.

None of what God did for us was by our merit, it is our free gift of salvation and means we have relationship with our Savior. We can only choose to respond and embrace it. As you come before him in prayer, recognize that even the right to approach God is a gift from him. Thank him for breaking down the divide between you and him. Praise him for the freedom and confidence he has filled you with.

Father, I am so blessed to serve a God who takes an interest in his creation.

DAY 26

Mindset of Christ

In your relationships with one another, have the same mindset as Christ Jesus: Who, being in very nature God, did not consider equality with God something to be used to his own advantage and being found in appearance as a man, he humbled himself by becoming obedient to death— even death on a cross!

Philippians 2:5-6, 8 NIV

The attitude Christ bore was one of servanthood and sacrifice. His humble obedience is meant to serve as a model for us to replicate. If the King of the universe is willing to overlook his grandiose rights for the sake of love, and subject himself to all the mistreatment of the world, then we can also partake in serving others in the relationships God has given us.

Whatever our current calling, we know we are walking with a God who understands. He can help you embrace the relationships he has given you with the same attitude he has for others. You can love others the way he has loved you when you do it through his strength.

God, help me to embrace a humble and obedient mindset as I serve you.

DAY 27

Compassion and Justice

The Lord longs to be gracious to you;
therefore he will rise up to show you compassion.
For the Lord is a God of justice.
Blessed are all who wait for him!
Isaiah 30:18 NIV

The beautiful blending of God's compassion and justice is what gives us the hope that he will amend everything in his timing. We long for his justice now, but he compassionately holds back his judgment a while longer.

This same compassion forgave our sins and showed us grace when we were worthy of death. God's amazing grace lifts us back up. We wait patiently for the Lord because we know his grace is abounding and his fairness is exact.

Thank you, God, for the grace you have shown me every moment of my life.

DAY 28

MIRACULOUS

You are the God who does miracles;
you have shown people your power.
PSALM 77:14 NCV

The Bible is full of exciting accounts of power, healing, and resurrection. We find ourselves wishing that we had been there when the fire of God fell upon Elijah's sacrifice, or when the storm was stilled by a voice, or when the blind man gained sight, or when Lazarus stepped out of the tomb.

God is clear that miracles didn't stop when the Bible ended. His power isn't limited by the ages, and he is just as omnipotent today as he always has been. Approach this day with hope in your heart. God is a God of the impossible.

God, I believe in the miracles you did in the Bible. Help me to believe that you still do miracles today.

There is always a greater plan at work.

DAY 29

TRUE LIFE

This is how God showed his love to us: He sent his one and only Son into the world so that we could have life through him.

1 JOHN 4:9 NCV

The Bible is so clear that Jesus is God's Son and that true life is found only through him. It says that God sent him, implying that he came here from elsewhere. Jesus was not simply born here like the rest of us; he existed before time with God and as God. They are one together and divine in nature.

Being sent also indicates that Jesus had been given a mission. He was not on a casual visit to earth, but on an assignment to demonstrate God's love for us, his complete dominance over death and all evil realms, and to free us from every form of bondage by taking it on himself.

God, thank you that your love is more than a feeling. You demonstrate it with action. I want to do the same.

DAY 30

LIFE IN CHRIST

If there is any encouragement in Christ, any comfort in love, any participation in the Spirit, any affection and sympathy, complete my joy by being of the same mind, having the same love, being in full accord and of one mind.

PHILIPPIANS 2:1-2 ESV

The cause and effect outlined in these verses speak to the relevance of the love of Christ and, as consequence, Christian love. Christ is our encouragement and his love comforts us. The Holy Spirit guides us and is involved in our lives. Anyone who has accepted Christ as their Savior is well acquainted with his affection and sympathy.

The next verse relates the clear outcome of such moralities: we will experience joy, love, and have a similar mindset as other believers which unites us under Christ. This letter was written to the Philippians so long ago, and yet the same truths are evident in our lives today. Praise God for being the completion of our love, joy, and unity.

God, thank you for being the completion of love, joy, and unity.

DAY 31

SOURCE OF STRENGTH

Be strong in the Lord and in his mighty power.

EPHESIANS 6:10 NLT

Paul did not undercut the importance of the spiritual battles we engage with. He wrote often about how we are in a war against evil and cautioned us to be alert to it. Just prior to describing a detailed metaphor of suiting up in spiritual armor with each of its specific components, he gave the most necessary piece of battleplan advice: "Be strong in the Lord."

God is ready and willing to give us everything we need for any situation. Often, however, he will wait for us to ask so we are reminded that he is our source of strength and that we should always be turned toward him.

God , I look to you for the battleplans for life. Thank you that you have not hidden them from me.

DAY 32

Ask and Receive

"Keep on asking, and you will receive what you ask for. Keep on seeking, and you will find. Keep on knocking, and the door will be opened to you."

Matthew 7:7 NLT

The disciples had obviously asked God for many things before Jesus uttered these words. However, Jesus had been with them on earth. He had not yet accomplished on the cross what he came to earth to do, he had not stood as mediator before God for us, the veil had not yet been torn, and the Holy Spirit had not been given to us.

Christ's death and resurrection provided the way for us to approach God once again because our sins had been forgiven. The Holy Spirit came to help guide us in the way we should go, and he reforms our minds to be one with Christ. When we pray and our hearts are aligned with his, God will surely give us everything we need.

Father, thank you that when I ask for what is on your heart, you will answer my prayers.

The right to approach God is a gift from him.

DAY 33

Encourage Others

Encourage one another and build one another up, just as you are doing.

1 Thessalonians 5:11 NASB

The events of life and the digression of the world should not shock us or cause us to panic. Instead, the realization that one day we will go home to Jesus should encourage us and reassure us through the dismal times. We are called upon to share that encouragement with other believers so they too can be motivated to endure.

As we edify others, may it be with a heart that yearns to see them prosper in their life with the Lord. As each person is different, so how they become motivated will be different. We need to listen and learn from the Lord regarding his creations. Then, let us humbly serve other believers, provide them comfort, and spur them on in their faith.

God, please show me how I can serve someone else in your family today.

DAY 34

WONDERFULLY MADE

I praise you because I am fearfully and wonderfully made;
your works are wonderful,
I know that full well.
PSALM 139:14 NIV

The Father created us in his image for his purpose with much care and consideration. We should be careful not to complain about the handiwork of God, but to praise him for his wonderful design. He is worthy of admiration not resentment and criticism.

Taking care of ourselves can be a way of respecting God for his gift but rejecting the wonderful way he made us by hating who we are is unappreciative. We should consider how the Lord delights in us and how he created us for his pleasure. Rather than comparing ourselves to others, we can ask for his eyes to see the way he does. We can revel in our unique and wonderful design while giving him all the glory and praise.

Father, as I seek to improve myself, may it be out of care for what you have given me and not out of contempt for your design.

DAY 35

Everlasting Love

*"I have loved you with an everlasting love;
I have drawn you with unfailing kindness."*
Jeremiah 31:3 NIV

The Israelites often turned away from God in favor of other idols or of themselves. Then, when they faced persecution, they would run back to the Lord. Over and over, he received them back. He does not turn aside a contrite heart. True repentance should not present only when help is needed, but the Lord understood the weakness of the Israelites and continued to welcome them home, showing them unfailing kindness.

Even when your faith is weak, the Lord will accept you if you ask. He helps you to mature in faith and gives you ample amounts of grace. His love is everlasting and his compassion is certain. His mercy is undeniable. Thank him for forgiving your sins again and again, for calling you back to him, and for treating you as a true heir of his kingdom.

Father, when I try to forge my own way, please draw me back to you.

DAY 36

The Lord's Delight

His pleasure is not in the strength of the horse,
nor his delight in the legs of the warrior;
the Lord delights in those who fear him,
who put their hope in his unfailing love.

Psalm 147:10-11 niv

The Lord is not lacking in strength; our show of power does not impress him. He wants us to learn how to trust in him and rely on his might rather than attempt to muscle our way through life in our own strength. Humility is far more pleasing to the Lord than ability. Our skills and strength are gifts from God, and our humble love is our grateful gift back to him.

Both the mighty horse and the tender butterfly were created by God, both are cared for by God, and both reflect a side of his character. Even if we feel confident and capable, we ought to fear God and follow his leadership. This will be pleasing to the Lord and will keep us out of a lot of potential trouble.

God, thank you that you display both your strength and your tenderness in my life.

You can love others the way God has loved you when you do it through his strength.

DAY 37

Condemnation

"Do not judge others, and you will not be judged. Do not condemn others, or it will all come back against you. Forgive others, and you will be forgiven."

Luke 6:37 NLT

The Lord requires his children to extend grace toward others, since he covered us with his grace. He judged us innocent because Christ paid for our sins. Yet, if we judge others, then we choose to relinquish God's forgiving verdict of us. As soon as we condemn others by holding them to their sins, we condemn ourselves and all our sins will be held against us.

To overlook God's command on how we should love one another is to decline God's love for us. His love is unchanging, but he will withhold his grace from those who withhold it from others. His Word is clear. The choice is ours.

God, it's hard not to judge other people. Help me to realize that as I judge them, I am being judged. I want to show forgiveness instead.

DAY 38

PATH OF LIFE

The path of the righteous is like the morning sun, shining ever brighter till the full light of day.

PROVERBS 4:18 NIV

The path to life can be treacherous at times. It often leads us places we do not like to go. However, there is joy found in the journey. Not only are there eternal pleasures stored up for those who remain faithful, but there are rewards here now for following God. The greatest of these rewards is that we grow closer to God the more we walk with him. We understand his love, his character, and his plan better because we have a relationship with him.

Following God is the only path that leads to true and lasting life. When we stay the course, he fills us with joy, makes his presence known, and leads us every step of the way.

Thank you, God, for the eternal pleasures you have promised to those who faithfully follow you.

DAY 39

Protection

Let all who take refuge in you be glad;
let them ever sing for joy.
Spread your protection over them,
that those who love your name may rejoice in you.

Psalm 5:11 niv

The remarkable grace God gives us provides impenetrable protection and insatiable joy! Since we love the Lord so much, his protection makes us glad and we rejoice in it. If we did not understand God, we would likely not appreciate his protection. We would fight against his laws and act out in disobedience. Then, we would also be vulnerable to all the enemy's attacks and all the elements of the world.

The Lord's protection does not guarantee that we will be spared from pain or sadness. It is a safety much more lasting, protecting our hearts from failing and keeping our feet on the path that leads to life. Those who do not understand will attempt to build their own barricade, but for those of us who realize what God's grace entails, we have every reason to rejoice.

God, I am so thankful for the protection you have placed over my life. I rejoice in you.

DAY 40

The Great Escape

The Lord brought his people out of Egypt,
loaded with silver and gold;
and not one among the tribes of Israel even stumbled.

Psalm 105:37 NLT

The story of Israel's rescue from hundreds of years of slavery in Egypt is not to be thought of lightly. What a miracle that God's chosen people were finally delivered. There were generations after generations that were born and died in slavery, and finally this was the generation that God set free. Not only were they set free, but he loaded them with silver and gold and made it easy for them to escape.

Sometimes these stories seem so far away in history that we don't relate to them. We need to remind ourselves that God is the God of yesterday, today, and forever. He is as present this day as he was with his people hundreds of years ago. What a powerful God we serve!

God, you are awesome. Thank you for helping me to escape from the things that are not good for me.

Approach this day with hope in your heart.

DAY 41

Natural Response

Bear with each other, and forgive each other. If someone does wrong to you, forgive that person because the Lord forgave you.

Colossians 3:13 NCV

We should be quick to forgive and to help others succeed. If we truly understand what Christ did for us and what he saved us from, then forgiveness would be our natural response. Everything we have is because of the grace of God poured on us, so we are to show each other the same grace.

This verse is not instructing us to be apathetic toward sin or stay silent in the face of injustice but to forgive the wrongs done to us and help others to bear the burdens of their weaknesses. This way, growth can occur and the grace we have been shown is made evident by the way we show grace to others.

God, thank you for your forgiveness. I want to forgive others as you have forgiven me.

DAY 42

Sweet Dreams

Fully awake, he rebuked the storm and shouted to the sea, "Hush! Calm down!" All at once the wind stopped howling and the water became perfectly calm.

Mark 4:39 TPT

The wind picked up and seemed to come from all directions. The boat began to rock. Lightning lit the pitch-black sky, thunder rumbled, and rain pelted. The disciples should have been sleeping, but they couldn't with the storm raging all around them. In fact, they were so anxious about the weather that they actually thought they might lose their lives that night.

Stressful situations and events can cause temporary insomnia. The disciples worried about a violent storm and couldn't close their eyes. We can also worry about storms in our lives. Sleep is important to our bodies for obvious reasons, but lack of sleep can create anxiety, and anxiety can lead to lack of sleep. We need to be careful not to fall into a vicious cycle with one begetting the other. Troubles may surround us, but Jesus never leaves us nor forsakes us.

Thank you, Jesus, that you are with me in the storm. You will not let me drown.

DAY 43

Look Up

Let us run with endurance the race God has set before us.

Hebrews 12:1 NLT

The writer of Hebrews compares our Christian journey to that of running a race. When we run a race, particularly a long one, we need perseverance to not quit when it gets hard. Races often start out feeling quite manageable, but inevitably there comes a point when completing the race seems not only daunting but perhaps impossible.

When this happens, it seems like the runner's eyes lower to the ground and rest on the monotony of watching one foot after the other slowly propel them forward. When you watch the ground while running, your distance gained is almost imperceptible. However, when you look up, toward your goal, you become reinvigorated to endure and persist. Your call as a runner is to fix your eyes on God. If you watch the ground or look behind you, you'll grow weary. But eyes staid on him will give you all the strength you need.

God, help me to fix my eyes on you. I need your strength.

DAY 44

BURNING THE CANDLE

It is in vain that you rise up early and go late to rest,
eating the bread of anxious toil;
for he gives to his beloved sleep.

PSALM 4:8 NIV

There are days where you might wake up a little more sluggish, with a little less energy and positivity about the day. That can feel kind of empty, a gap you're hoping to fill.

The great thing about the God you serve is that in him you can be complete. He can be the gap filler. As you sit with him, his light begins to burn brighter. When it's hard to get out of bed because you feel anxious or worried about the day ahead, ask God for the energy and strength to face another day. He will give you what you need.

God, help me not to burn the candle at both ends. I need time for rest and connection with you.

God's love is everlasting, his compassion is certain, and his mercy is undeniable.

DAY 45

Well Timed

Everyone enjoys giving great advice.
But how delightful it is to say the right thing
at the right time!

Proverbs 15:23 TPT

There are situations in life where you feel lost for words. Often this is in moments of deep grief, sudden shock, or extreme surprise. Overwhelming emotions can be hard to express and when someone shares these emotions with us, we don't always know how to reply. The Bible speaks a lot about being slow to speak, so God doesn't expect us to know what to say immediately.

An appropriate response to someone doesn't have to be quick, it's just good if it's timely. The next time you find yourself lost for words, give yourself time to think and pray about a response. There's wisdom in letting the Holy Spirit guide you with encouraging words. Think of the joy you can bring to someone, perhaps not instantly, but in time, with the right words.

God, please give me encouraging words for people when it is the right time for them to hear.

DAY 46

Peaceful Sleep

I lie down and sleep;
I wake again, because the Lord sustains me.

Psalm 3:3-4 niv

There is always something to worry about, isn't there? Whether it's health, finances, relationships, or details, there are many unknowns in life that can easily keep us worrying. What if we could trust completely that God would take care of us and our loved ones. God is our rock and he alone will sustain us.

There will be many unknowns in your life. There will be moments when the rug feels as though it's been pulled out from under you and there is nothing to do but despair. In those moments that you can't control, you can trust. You can rest your soul, your mind, and your body in the hands of the one who has the power to sustain you.

God, thank you that even in the unknowns, I can rest in the knowledge that you will sustain me.

DAY 47

Overcome the World

"I have told you these things, so that in me you may have peace. In this world you will have trouble. But take heart! I have overcome the world."

John 16:33 NIV

There is no evil in this world that Christ has not already overcome. He has accounted for everything that may happen to us and guarantees that we can overcome it through his power. We can take heart and have confidence knowing that we also have secured victory because of the Lord Jesus' resurrection.

God has related his plan to us so we may have peace knowing that our future with him is guaranteed. Regardless of what terrible situations we face in this life, they will pass away. Christ's kingdom is lasting and his victory is forever.

God, when trials shake my peace and cause me to doubt, I look to you. You can help me overcome everything that comes my way.

DAY 48

POWER WITHOUT LIMIT

To him who is able to do immeasurably more than all we ask or imagine, according to his power that is at work within us, to him be glory in the church and in Christ Jesus throughout all generations, for ever and ever! Amen.

EPHESIANS 3:20-21 NIV

There is only so much that we can accomplish in our own strength. We plow through our tasks, and we can get a lot done. But we are limited in our power.

God has no limit in what he can do! If we ask him to work in our lives, there's no stopping the amazing things that will happen! We can accomplish more than we'd ever think to ask for. The best part is that he wants to do it for us. It's not a chore for him or another task to cross off his list so that you'll stop pestering him.

God, I am asking for bigger and bolder things today. Thank you for the supernatural ability to accomplish all that is before me.

Following God is the only path that leads to true and lasting life.

DAY 49

MY SHEEP

"I am the good shepherd. The good shepherd lays down his life for the sheep."
JOHN 10:11 NIV

There is something soothing about the thought of sheep and shepherds, unless of course you are the one tending sheep. Herding, calling, feeding, leading, and gathering can't be all that easy. After all, aren't people a lot like sheep, and isn't life full of shepherding? Wouldn't it be nice at the end of a day to gather all our cares and leave them inside a pen to stay put for the night? Like scattered sheep, tasks leap through our minds. Herding our daily strivings into a safe and protected place and depositing them there would be lovely.

Jesus offered himself as the only way into the sheepfold. He gave us his Word to guide us and lead our steps. When the cares of our lives scatter through our nights like restless leaping sheep, God wants us to remember who blocks the doorway. No one guards and protects like he does. We can rest easy in his sheepfold.

Thank you, Jesus, that you are my good shepherd. Help me to rest in your safety.

DAY 50

HIDING

Where can I go from your Spirit?
Where can I flee from your presence?
PSALM 139:7 NIV

These words were probably very similar to the ones Adam and Eve used in the garden when they were ashamed of their disobedience. It's how we feel when we are ashamed of something that we have done wrong. We want to hide and we don't want to be found!

It's okay to feel bad about doing the wrong thing and to feel guilty about making a wrong decision. But you can't live in that guilt and you can't hide forever. God already knows where you are. He is seeking restoration with you. His Spirit is already with you. If you are trying to run from him it's a losing battle! Instead, surrender to him and let his grace bring you joy.

God, I run to you over and over again. Help me not to hide in shame but to turn to you.

DAY 51

Exaltation

"Be still, and know that I am God.
I will be exalted among the nations,
I will be exalted in the earth!"

Psalm 46:10 esv

This psalm is not an invitation to be lazy, but to heed God. Children of God are expected to work hard, be responsible, and fulfill their duties. We are not, however, to frantically attempt to force our way through life ourselves, without heeding the Word of God or accepting his help and intervention.

When we rely on the power of our own strength, the temptation is to exalt ourselves. God is our source of strength, and he alone is to be exalted in the earth. He may choose at times to honor us as a good father does, but we should be glorifying him and recognizing his leadership in our lives.

God, help me today to spend time listening to you.

DAY 52

APPROACHING GOD

This is the confidence we have in approaching God: that if we ask anything according to his will, he hears us.

1 JOHN 5:14 NIV

This verse should vanquish any idea Christians may have of God simply being a wishing well. Tossing prayers up to heaven and hoping for our own desires to be fulfilled is not how lovestruck, servant-hearted believers are expected to approach the Almighty.

When our deepest desire is for the Lord and for all people to come to know him, we pray to him for directions and answers that align with his agenda. That does not mean we have to vet our prayers or leave out details and requests that matter to us, but that everything comes under a covering of a mutual understanding that his master plan is what we are aiming at and hoping for above all else.

God, show me what is on your heart and mind today. I want to pray according to your will.

Your call as a runner is to fix your eyes on God.

DAY 53

WHATEVER COMES

I will be strength to him
and I will give him my grace
to sustain him no matter what comes.

PSALM 89:21 TPT

This verse was God's promise to David when he chose him to be the king of Israel. We have the hindsight to know the mistakes and troubles that David went through. Scripture tells us David's story of blessing, sin, consequence, joy, battles, fear, and love.

David went through a lot in his life and the truth of this verse prevailed. God gave him grace and sustained him no matter what came. Let this verse be your promise today. Trust God to shower you with grace that will sustain you through everything you face today.

Father, today I choose to walk in confidence no matter what comes.

DAY 54

LIFE'S JOURNEY

Surely you have granted him unending blessings and made him glad with the joy of your presence.

PSALM 21:6 NIV

Though we commonly associate the words *fear* and *fright* with one another, they don't mean the same thing. Having a fear of the Lord means we respect him. It means we are in awe of him. He is, in fact, a God of great joy. When we seek to be fully in his presence, we can find that joy.

Our Father wants you to experience his joy. Unending blessings? Let's sign up for that! Shake off any old notions of dread or apprehension you may feel about being in his presence and seek the path of life he has set for you. He is a source of great delight. Rejoice in that knowledge today.

God, your unending goodness brings joy to my life. Thank you for the blessing of being with you.

DAY 55

Self-Control

Better to be patient than powerful;
better to have self-control than to conquer a city.
Proverbs 16:32 NLT

What benefit is it to conquer a city if the other city had better intentions? If the Lord were to select someone to do a job, would it not make more sense that he chooses the one who is willing to listen to him and patiently wait for his instructions over the one who is more powerful?

Our power and our strength come from God as does our calling. Enacting skills he has given us brashly and arrogantly is unfitting for a child of God. He has equipped us in order to obey him. Therefore, having self-control and patiently waiting upon the Lord's instructions is of more worth than spoils from an entire city.

Lord, please show me how I can use my gifts and talents for the best possible outcomes.

DAY 56

REJOICE

Rejoice in the Lord always. I will say it again: Rejoice!
PHILIPPIANS 4:4 CSB

True joy is so much more than mere happiness. As Christians, we rejoice because of the hope we have in Jesus. There will come a day when all our suffering and sorrows will be wiped away and we will finally be at home with our Lord. Understanding this powerful truth should fill us with a continual joy that is more real than our circumstances.

We should not overlook that when Paul penned these words, he was in jail for being wrongly accused. Just prior to his imprisonment, he had been shipwrecked, bitten by a snack, and placed under house arrest. Yet because of how aware he was of his eternal inheritance, nothing was able to steal his joy.

God, your joy in my life is so important. Help me to draw from that joy when things are difficult and when they are not.

In those moments that you can't control, you can trust.

DAY 57

UNFATHOMABLE

He will not grow tired or weary,
and his understanding no one can fathom.
ISAIAH 40:28 NIV

God never grows weary of doing good, not does he tire of loving us. He is the Creator of the universe, and he diligently upholds the world, governs it wisely, and judges it righteously. With vigor and strength, he provides for all his creation, from the birds to the grass to his beloved Church.

With an unfathomable understanding and infinite love that none could begin to grasp, he cares for all our needs out of his goodness. He understands each of us, considers our desires, and gives us all a unique calling. He is majestic and his ways are perfect. He has crafted everything with care and consideration. His eyes are always on us and he leads us in the path of righteouness. He is a good God who never grows weary.

God, you are near, and you are good. Thank you for never growing tired of loving me.

DAY 58

Let Grace Win

If you bite and devour each other, watch out or you will be destroyed by each other.

Galatians 5:15 NIV

Watching animals in the wild hunt, defend, and fight for territory can be brutal. We are not wild animals, but it might pay to stop and think about whether we are acting like them. When we start to assume or say unkind things about people, it can be the start of an attack on character or a judgment of the way things are being done.

God doesn't call us to be the judge of what others say or do; he wants us to have control of ourselves. Instead of being ready to attack or defend our territory, we should be quick to forgive. Always let grace win. Let your heart be full of it so it spills over into the way you treat others.

God, please forgive me for speaking unfairly about others and bring healing into those places where I have been hurt.

DAY 59

A Pilgrimage

How blessed is the man whose strength is in You,
in whose heart are the highways to Zion!
Psalm 84:5 NASB

We are a go, go, go culture. We keep it running 24/7 as fast as we can. Do you have the courage to slow down? Too many of us are plagued by fear of missing out. This fear grips us to take life more at the speed of a motocross race and less the way it was intended to be: a pilgrimage. An exodus out of bondage and into freedom. Out of darkness, into light. Out of death, into resurrection. A pilgrimage is a slower journey, not a race run at remarkable speed.

We run quickly for two reasons: either we don't want to miss out, or we want to hurry up and get past all the hard stuff. You won't be rewarded for how fast you obtain the prize, or how much you accomplished along the way. On this exodus, quality matters. Miss out. Say no. Go slower. Don't give in to the temptation to run. Walk with Christ, allowing him to mature you as you move.

God, when my pace is too quick, remind me to slow down and rest in you.

DAY 60

NOT DESTROYED

We are hard pressed on every side, but not crushed; perplexed, but not in despair; persecuted, but not abandoned; struck down, but not destroyed.

2 CORINTHIANS 4:8-9 NIV

We are God's treasure in jars of clay. The Holy Spirit lives in us and enables us to have the power to accomplish all the Lord has called us to. This strength did not originate with us, but with the Spirit, and so our lives testify of God.

Just as jars of clay are, we may be battered and bruised in life. We may even shatter! But the treasure that is within is unbreakable. No matter what happens, we are not crushed, we do not despair, and we are never abandoned. What God has fashioned and redeemed cannot be destroyed.

Thank you, God, that you have made me eternally indestructible. I trust your design!

When we seek to be fully in God's presence, we find joy.

DAY 61

No More Tears

You have delivered my soul from death,
my eyes from tears, my feet from stumbling.
Psalm 116:8 esv

We are promised a time where there will be no more death, tears, or stumbling. This life is full of hardships, but we can live in hope that a day will come where joy will reign supreme. It is this hope that carries us through the hard times when we trust that God is still good and that he has good plans for us now and especially in the life to come.

Try to bravely face this day with joy concerning your future. This is not where it ends! Look forward to an eternity of joy, where the pain of this life will be no more. Thank God that even today he can bring relief to your physical pain, healing to your emotional pain, and restoration to your spiritual weakness. Lean on him through the hard times and he will give you strength to live with eternity in mind.

Thank you, Father, for the day when there will be no more tears and sadness. I look forward to that.

DAY 62

Deep Contentment

I don't say this out of need, for I have learned to be content in whatever circumstances I find myself.

Philippians 4:11 CSB

We can close our eyes and rest with ease when our worlds are in perfect harmony. It is easy to find peace in peaceful times. Happiness is at our fingertips and our steps are light. In these seasons, it is effortless to raise our faces to the sky and say "Alleluia," and to declare God's goodness. The struggle comes, though, when life isn't easy. When we are surrounded by heartbreak and disappointment. When grief feels suffocating, and hope seems so far away. When every day, even every moment seems impossible.

We forget in these times that true contentment, true joy, is still in our reach. We just have to open up our eyes and hearts to it. When we learn to see joy in every circumstance, we are able to step bravely into each day set before us. Our circumstances do not define us; rather, joy becomes so rooted and engrained in who we are that finding peace becomes our second nature.

God, thank you for your true contentment and genuine peace.

DAY 63

EVEN BEFORE THAT

Your eyes saw my unformed body;
all the days ordained for me were written in your book
before one of them came to be.
PSALM 139:16 NIV

We celebrate our birthdays as the day that our fully formed body came into the world and we breathed our first breath. Birthdays mark the beginning of our lives, but in this Scripture, God was celebrating you long before your birthday. He saw you before you were even formed; he knew that you were destined for life, even before that first breath. What an amazing God we have, who is not only all-knowing, but ever personal.

Take courage and strength from the truth that you were destined from the beginning and you have a wonderful purpose. Whatever you may be about to face in your day, hold your head high and remember the one who created you for such a time as this.

Thank you, Creator God, that your attention is fixed on me. You have never taken your eyes off me.

DAY 64

ENCOURAGING BRAVERY

When I am afraid, I will trust you.
I praise God for his word.
I trust God, so I am not afraid.
What can human beings do to me?

PSALM 56:3-4 NCV

We hear parents admonish their children not to be afraid. The older we get, the more there seems to be afraid of. Who can you encourage today, not by telling them to not be afraid, but by asking them to be brave? Asking people to mask their fear will only work temporarily at best. Asking them to make a choice for bravery gives them confidence in God's character and care.

Don't stuff down what you are feeling and move on by your own strength. Be brave in the situations that strike fear in you, knowing that God is fighting for you. Who do you know that needs to hear this today? Let God use you as his vessel to bring freedom. Help others remove their masks and hand them the bravery banner.

God, please help me to walk in bravery today. I put my trust in you.

Instead of being ready to attack or defend your territory, be quick to forgive.

DAY 65

YOUR PEOPLE

Trust in him at all times, you people;
pour out your hearst before him.
God is our refuge.
PSALM 62:8 CSB

We like to spend time on our personal relationship with God, and yet there is more to our faith than just ourselves. We were created to be in community with one another and one really important benefit of a close community is that we can be encouraged, or encourage others, in times of distress.

Think of the last time you felt really anxious or discouraged and reflect on who you were able to share those feelings with. Together we can pour out our hearts to him. We are all on this journey, not just individually, but walking alongside each other. Take a moment today to encourage the people you are walking through life with.

Father, show me how I can be intentional about developing close relationships with those who encourage me in my faith.

DAY 66

SPIRITUAL DESTINATION

Blessed are those whose strength is in you,
whose hearts are set on pilgrimage.
PSALM 84:5 NIV

We never really arrive at our spiritual destination of holiness, and that's the way it is meant to be. The beauty is found where the heart is inclined toward finding the presence of God. This is our journey of faith in Christ. It is a pilgrimage in every sense of the word.

It might be a long and difficult terrain to navigate, but there will be wonders to see along the way and some profound insights and thoughts as you progress. This pilgrimage is one that ends at the most beautiful of places, one that your heart cannot fully comprehend. Enjoy the journey that you are on today.

God, I appreciate the beauty of my walk with you. Thank you for this amazing journey.

DAY 67

Uncomplicated Freedom

"I have swept away your offenses like a cloud,
your sins like the morning mist.
Return to me, for I have redeemed you."

Isaiah 44:22 NIV

We over-complicate freedom in the Christian life. Through our legalisms, we try to find a way to humanize the redeeming work of the cross because we simply can't wrap our minds around the supernatural character of God.

It can be hard to understand the complete grace offered at Calvary because we are incapable of giving that kind of grace. But when God says that he has forgotten our sin, and that he has made us new, he really means it. God is love, and love keeps no record of wrongs. Nothing can keep us from his love. Salvation tore the veil that separated us from the holiness of God. That complete work cannot be diminished or erased by anything we do.

Thank you, Father, for simple freedom. You have given me unlimited, undeserved grace.

DAY 68

POWERFUL VIRTUES

Do you think lightly of the riches of His kindness and tolerance and patience, not knowing that the kindness of God leads you to repentance?

ROMANS 2:4 NASB

We tend to think of kindness, tolerance, and patience as some of the softer emotions. Consider however, the tolerance of a mother giving birth to a newborn, sacrificing her body and emotions for the love of a child. Think of the patience of a sister who sits alongside her sibling in the darkest days of her depression. Think of a daughter who cares diligently for her dying parent.

None of those actions are soft or meek. Kindness, tolerance, and patience can be fiercely, fervently, and powerfully loving. These Scriptures suggest that God's kindness, tolerance, and patience is exactly that—powerful enough to lead us to change our ways and never look back. This is nothing to think lightly of; it is life changing!

God, you are so good. Your kindness compels me to change.

What God has fashioned and redeemed cannot be destroyed.

DAY 69

Beside Still Waters

He leads me beside still waters.

Psalm 23:2 ESV

Have you wondered why *still waters* are used in this psalm? Have you ever been by a quiet stream? The surface is so clear it's like a mirror. It reflects the peaceful beauty of God's creation. The water draws us to it and the silence and stillness invite us to also be motionless. Those still waters give us rest for our soul.

Can you think of anything that a stressed and grieving person could use more than calmness and restful silence? God knows what we need to restore our souls, to refresh us in our heartache. But it's hard to hear his words of comfort if we're zipping around, or if we're in turmoil and constant action. When we're still, we can hear God's soft whispers. We can draw close to the only one who can truly comfort an aching heart.

God, lead me beside still waters today. I need rest for my soul.

DAY 70

KEEPING A SECRET

A gossip goes around revealing a secret,
but a trustworthy person keeps a confidence.
PROVERBS 11:13 CSB

We've all been there before. A friend leans in and whispers, "Did you hear about what she did?" And something in us wants to be in the know. To hear the scoop. To spread the word. It's almost as if we are built to be mean girls. To share what we know of others' downfalls and fallacies.

It might feel good in the moment to tear people down because then we are not alone in the many ways we fall short. But it is a lie. We were designed to lift one another up. To be worthy of knowing a friend's secrets because we will keep the knowledge to ourselves. The next time you are tempted to share what isn't yours to tell, take a deep breath and pause. Ask yourself if betraying a confidence is worth letting down a friend. Instead, allow yourself to be the type of friend that the Lord has designed you to be.

God, please show me how I can be a trusted friend. I want to do a better job of this.

DAY 71

Bless Someone

May he give you the desire of your heart
and make all your plans succeed.
Psalm 20:4 NIV

What a beautiful Scripture to read. May God give you the desire of your heart and make your plans succeed. This is a great verse for you, but could it also be for someone else in your life? Think of someone in need of encouragement and choose to pray this blessing over that person.

It might be your mother or father, someone you know has been unwell, perhaps it's the friend with a new baby, or someone who has just started a new job. Whatever that person's situation is, pray that God would make their plans succeed!

God, please show me someone I can pray for today. I want them to succeed in their plan to serve you.

DAY 72

His Strength

Look to the Lord and his strength;
seek his face always.

Psalm 105:4 NIV

Our natural instinct is to cry out to God in a panic and desperately search for him when we find ourselves in crisis. However, we don't have to panic or feel distressed in the face of the unknown. We can just ask him for help and he will be faithful to meet us. His strength is readily available. We can know the joy of his presence and the comfort and stability of his faithfulness.

God calms our racing and anxious thoughts with truth. He offers us wisdom and direction in the middle of decision making. He pierces the darkness that preys on us with his light. He fills us with gratitude and thanksgiving and renews our faith. He breathes bravery into our weak and timid souls.

Thank you, God, that I can always draw strength from you.

You were destined from the beginning, and you have a wonderful purpose.

DAY 73

Hope

May the God of hope fill you with all joy and peace as you trust in him, so that you may overflow with hope by the power of the Holy Spirit

Romans 15:13 NIV

What differentiates hope from a wish? Think about the lottery. Does one hope to win, or wish to win? How about a promotion, a pregnancy, or a proposal? Both hoping and wishing contain desire, but for wishing, that is where it ends. Hope goes deeper. The strong desire for something good to happen is coupled with a reason to believe that it will.

We see then how vital hope is, and why it's such a beautiful gift. Desire without hope is empty, but together they bring joy, expectancy, and peace. When we put our hope in Christ, he becomes our reason to believe good things will happen. He is our hope.

Father, I believe good things will happen. You are my hope.

DAY 74

Righteous Answers

By awesome deeds you answer us with righteousness,
O God of our salvation,
the hope of all the ends of the earth
and of the farthest seas.

Psalm 65:5 ESV

What have you been asking of God lately? It could be healing from illness, prayer for someone close to you who is hurting, or maybe you just need a little help in your relationships. It is often said that God hears our prayers; yet you might feel like he has never answered yours.

God can seem very far away and unconcerned with your requests and needs. These feelings, however, are not the truth. The truth is that God is always very near to you. He knows your heart, he knows what you need, and he will answer. Trust him as you read this Scripture again and know that he will answer your prayers with amazing wonders and inspiring displays of power. Let this increase your faith today.

God, you are my hope that extends to the ends of the earth and farthest of seas.

DAY 75

A PLACE OF REST

The LORD is my shepherd; I shall not want.
He makes me lie down in green pastures.
PSALM 23:1 ESV

What is restful for you? Is there a place you like to go when you need to be refreshed? There's something special about enjoying the beauty of God's creation, and while we sit and take it in, we can almost feel the stress seeping away from us.

When we discover the beauty of creation—maybe a still lake, a canopy of leaves, a starry sky—a sweet peacefulness seeps into our souls. We find rest as we worship the one who is the author of beauty. Both our souls and bodies can be refreshed. Sometimes we don't have to get in our pajamas to find rest. We just need to look for Jesus. And when we find his fingerprints on the world he created, we need to make it a priority to spend time with him there, and discover rest for our souls.

Creator God, thank you for your beautiful creation that I can find so much joy in. Help me to look for it today.

DAY 76

THE DESIRE BENEATH

Since we know he hears us when we make our requests, we also know that he will give us what we ask for.

1 JOHN 5:15 NLT

When birthdays or anniversaries are coming up, we often get asked about what we want as a gift. You may be someone that answers that easily, or you might take a while. Eventually you have an answer of what you would like or even need, but you never really know if you are going to get it, and you often have to wait until that significant day to find out!

We should be confident that God hears us when we tell him what we want or need. Perhaps we haven't had the confidence to voice it, but he knows our heart anyway. Could we consider that God knows the true desire behind our requests, and that this real desire is what we end up getting? It's a thought that might be worth pondering today.

God, I ask you today for that special something I've been thinking about. Thank you for hearing me.

God breathes bravery into your weak and timid soul.

DAY 77

Praise Always

I have learned the secret of being content in any and every situation, whether well fed or hungry, whether living in plenty or in want. I can do all this through him who gives me strength.

Philippians 4:12-13 NIV

When life is good, it is easy to praise God. *My life is full of blessings,* we think to ourselves. *He is so good to me!* But what happens when life is hard? Do we continue to give him the glory when we're thrown curveball after curveball?

Regardless of our circumstance, whatever our situation, we need to continue to give him the praises he so richly deserves. A life lived alongside Christ doesn't mean it will be one free of pain, of discomfort, of tough times. But it does mean that we can find contentment in it anyway because we have him in our lives to turn to. Pray for contentment today, whatever your circumstance. There is no crisis that the Lord is not willing to walk you through. You can do anything with him at your side!

God, help me to be content today no matter what my circumstances are. You are always good.

DAY 78

YOUR BEST WORK

Whatever you do, work heartily, as for the Lord and not for men, knowing that from the Lord you will receive the inheritance as your reward. You are serving the Lord Christ.

COLOSSIANS 3:23-24 ESV

When our work is difficult, mundane, or thankless, we can remember that everything we do is for the Lord. Out of appreciation and love for him, we embrace every day's tasks with joy because we serve the King! Even if our toils are for a difficult boss or unappreciative children, our callings come from God and our rewards do as well. We ought to put our best effort into our daily grind, even if it seems to be devalued here on earth because it has always been for God and not for mere man.

When others attempt to destroy your efforts, undermine your work, or steal your success, continue you to serve with your whole heart because that is what God has called you to act. The end results are in his hands.

God, I trust you to bless my work. You are my reward.

DAY 79

Crown of Joy

Those the Lord has rescued will return.
They will enter Zion with singing;
everlasting joy will crown their heads.
Isaiah 51:11 NIV

When the Lord rescued the Israelites out of Babylon and led them back to their own land, Jerusalem, there was great rejoicing and singing! Their sorrow was replaced by joy, for they had served in captivity for a long time. It was not the first time God had rescued them from slavery; Egypt was still fresh in their history. It also will not be the last time the Lord will rescue his people and lead them to their promised land.

When the Lord returns for his people again, we will finally enter his eternal promised land. Our sorrow and crying will be forever replaced with everlasting joy and singing. God never forgets his people. He has always made a way for his children to return to him when they go astray.

Father God, help me to wear joy as my crown.

DAY 80

STRONG

"Be strong and courageous and do the work. Don't be afraid or discouraged, for the LORD God, my God, is with you. He will not fail you or forsake you."

1 CHRONICLES 28:20 NLT

When the work before us is daunting, we may rush through it or stall out in the process. Jesus has an answer for that. He says he will not fail you or forsake you. To fail you would be to give you an answer or technique that does not work for what you are supposed to be doing. To forsake you would be to walk away from you in your time of need.

If you truly believe God has done either of these to you, you really need to sit in the quiet with your Bible and an open heart toward God. He promises that if you seek him fully, you will find him. In doing this, you will eradicate faulty thinking and get back on your feet with the strength and courage to do what had once seemed daunting. Jesus is with you!

God, thank you for helping me through all the difficult times in my life. I trust you to continue to help me.

DAY 81

Surrender and Rest

"Come to me, all you who are weary and burdened, and I will give you rest."

Matthew 11:28 NIV

When we are faced with a problem our first instinct is to grab it and not let it go. We have this belief that if we hold onto it tightly, we have some sense of control. Often that sense is false. It creates anxiety and lets fear flourish. The more we struggle to hold on, the harder the situation becomes, and the more exhausting the fight.

The attitude that God wants us to have toward our problems is one of bravery. He asks us to choose surrender over having control. A huge part of that brave choice is having faith in him. By surrendering our fears and letting go of worry, we are trusting God. We can relax our grip, lift our eyes and hands to the sky, and breathe. No problem is too big or too difficult for God to handle. When we trust him, we can finally rest.

God, I trust you in every aspect of my life. I surrender even the difficult parts to you.

DAY 82

Graciousness

Kindness to the poor is a loan to the Lord;
and he will give a reward to the lender.
Proverbs 19:17 CSB

When we give to those who cannot repay us, it is as if we are giving straight to God. The way we demonstrate our love for the Lord is by loving each other. When we are gracious to others, God will be gracious to us. When we forgive others, God will forgive us. When we give to others without an expectation for compensation, the Lord will certainly remember and repay us for our faithfulness.

The Lord is tremendously generous; we cannot outgive him. He sees every good deed and will not forget the generosity and grace we show to others. It is as if we are loving him directly. Our love for God can spur us on to love others. Rather than looking for what we can get, we should consider what we can give. God will reveal to us the needs in others that he wants us to meet. And we can serve without expecting anything in return because God sees and he will reward us.

God, I want to give to those who cannot repay me. Show me who that might be in my life.

Relax your grip, lift your eyes to the sky, and breathe.

DAY 83

The Good Lane

I am certain that I will see the Lord's goodness
in the land of the living.

Psalm 27:13 CSB

Do you ever catch yourself dwelling on the negative aspects of life? We can be nonchalant when someone tells us good news, but talk for hours about conflict, worries, and disappointment.

It is good to communicate things that aren't going so well in our lives, but we can also fall into the trap of setting our minds on the wrong things. Give your mind over to truth, honor, pure and lovely things today. You are sure to find goodness in unexpected places! Thank God for creating you with goodness in your heart.

God, please help me to avoid the temptation of indulging in negative talk today. You are better.

DAY 84

TIME TO EAT

They soon forgot what he had done
and did not wait for his plan to unfold.
PSALM 106:13 NIV

When you are asked about what you had for breakfast, can you even remember? With minds that are often full of so many things, forgetfulness can threaten to derail your appointments, friendships, and even your relationship with Jesus. It's not that Jesus will ever depart from you, but if you quickly forget the good and gracious things he has done, you are less likely to spend time communicating with him.

It is often in our moments of greatest joy that we forget about the source of that joy. Give yourself some space today to remember Jesus and what he has done in your life. Thank him for all the times he has provided you with wisdom, peace, and assurance. Be grateful for the provision of a roof over your head and people around you that care for you.

God, I want to remember your goodness every single day of my life. There is no end to your blessings.

DAY 85

Second Opinion

When my enemies retreat,
they stumble and perish before you.
Psalm 9:3 CSB

When you go to the doctor about a condition that needs explaining, you might not always be confident in their diagnosis. People will usually encourage you to get a second opinion. There are times when significant people in your life have told you something about yourself that makes you feel terrible. They might have labelled you as selfish, or crazy, or any number of accusations.

This is your time to get a second opinion, so go straight to your heavenly Father and ask him what he thinks. This is your God, who created you and loves you unconditionally and sees nothing but the best, redeemed person that you are.

God, I trust you to put my accusers to shame. You will show up and cover me.

DAY 86

Gems

Oil and incense bring joy to the heart,
and the sweetness of a friend is better than self-counsel.
PROVERBS 27:9 CSB

When you sign up for a competitive team sport, you have a basic understanding that you're going to have to work hard and that emotions will run high to win and succeed. You know that you'll win some, you'll lose some, and that somewhere along the way you'll start to feel good about playing the game whether you win or lose.

Playing a competitive team sport can sometimes feel the same as building relationships with other women. We win some—forming incredible relationships—and others we lose. We were created uniquely, and while we are asked to love one another, it doesn't mean that we hope for a best-friend relationship with each woman we meet.

God, thank you for friends who hold me accountable and also lift me up when I need it. They are treasures from you.

DAY 87

JESUS REP

Whatever you do, whether in word or deed, do it all in the name of the Lord Jesus, giving thanks to God the Father through him.

COLOSSIANS 3:17 NIV

When you work for a company or organization, you are expected to represent that particular brand or identity. Organizations who have a good reputation typically have a culture that their people are committed to being a part of. When you think of that company or brand, you can identify a certain value.

When you become a follower of Jesus, you also become his representative. Your personal relationship with Christ will inspire you to express something of his love, goodness, and grace to the world around you. You don't always need to shout that you are doing things in his name, you just need to simply be aware that your words and actions are influenced by his grace. Be encouraged today that you will represent him wherever you go.

God, please show me what part of you I am representing well and what I might need to let shine a little brighter.

DAY 88

VICTORY IN CHRIST

The God of peace will soon crush Satan under your feet. The grace of our Lord Jesus be with you.

ROMANS 16:20 NIV

As we continue to follow the ways of truth and godliness, the enemy also persists in his attempts to thwart us. Paul warned the people of false teachers and doctrine, which is one of the devil's crafty ways of undermining the work of Christ and Christians. God gives us the promise, however, that these attacks will ultimately fail and our enemy will be struck down! Everything that is a lie will fall away and only what is true will remain.

Through all of life's trials and the deception of others, we are given the promise that Jesus' grace will be with us. All the calamity and lies of the world cannot derail us from following Christ when we have been given the gifts of grace, peace, and truth.

Thank you, God, that I have victory in my life because of the work that Jesus did on the cross.

Rather than looking for what you can get, consider what you can give.

DAY 89

SECURE FEELING

If you lie down, you will not be afraid;
when you lie down, your sleep will be sweet.
PROVERBS 3:24 ESV

Sweet sleep, that goal after a day filled with hectic schedules and cramped expectations, dissipates with the fast drumbeat of a fearful heart. We've all been there, eyes wide-open staring into a dark room, ears strained for sound, and our breath held. Insecurity pins us like a blanket wrapped too tight until bit by bit we feel ourselves relax again.

Proverbs talks about security resulting from God's wisdom. As we incorporate the Word of God into our lives, God brings a different kind of security. Not the type we install with alarms or pay big money for, but the kind that underlies our thoughts and actions. God's security assures us as we end our day. He has walked with us during the hours past and will accompany us in the night ahead.

Thank you, Father, that you look out for me. You watch over me and keep me safe.

DAY 90

MATURE IN HIM

"The LORD, the LORD, the compassionate and gracious God, slow to anger, abounding in love and faithfulness."

EXODUS 34:6 NIV

Each day we walk with the Lord, we hope to mature in him. The more we learn about his character, his goodness and compassion, his mercy and his love, the more we yearn to be like him. It makes no difference whether you are a relatively new Christian or have been serving him for a long life. The more you know of God and his lovingkindness, the more convinced you are to better yourself. To soften your heart. To be like him.

What more could we want in our heart of hearts than to be compassionate and gracious? Slow to anger? Abounding in love and faithfulness? Looking into our own character is not always enjoyable. We tend to be selfish and prideful. We may be ashamed of things we have said or done. God is faithful to forgive us for yesterday and before.

God, please help me to be compassionate and gracious with those around me.

DAY 91

Worthy

You are worthy, our Lord and God, to receive glory and honor and power, for you created all things, and by your will they were created and have their being.

Revelation 4:11 niv

Within the vision God gave to John, he saw twenty-four elders before the throne of God. They were declaring the truths written in this verse. From God alone and for God alone do we exist and have a purpose. We are not an accident or an afterthought.

Creator God designed this world with all its wonder because it was his will. It is his will that we live, and he is therefore worthy of the praise of our lives. All glory, honor, and power are his, for we are nothing without him. Give him the honor he is due. Demonstrate the gratitude that you feel. God created you and gave you meaning. Uncover his purposes and declare his praises, for it is why you were made!

God, thank you for creating me with purpose—to declare your goodness and glory! I honor you today because you are worthy.

DAY 92

His Story

I will tell about the Lord's kindness and praise him for everything he has done. I will praise the Lord for the many good things he has given us and for his goodness to the people of Israel. He has shown great mercy to us and has been very kind to us.

Isaiah 63:7 NCV

You have a story to tell. When you think back over the years, reflect on the things that revealed God's goodness, graciousness, and love. Perhaps it was an illness or healing, a relationship or a relationship breakdown, it might have been a joy or a disappointment in your career. God is right next to us in all the things that life throws at us.

You may not have recognized him at the time, but hopefully you can attest to his kindness as you remember how you got through those times. This is your story and just like the Israelites, it is worth telling and repeating. Your story is important, so be brave and speak it out!

God, please help me to practice telling my story of your goodness, so you can be made known to many.

DAY 93

GRACE UPON GRACE

Of His fullness we have all received, and grace upon grace.

JOHN 1:16 NASB

You know those days, the perfect ones? Your hair looks great, you nail a work assignment (whether client presentation, spreadsheet, or getting twins to nap at the same time), you say just the right thing and make someone's day, and then come home to find dinner waiting for you. It's good upon good, blessing upon blessing.

Being a daughter of the Almighty gains us access to that blessed feeling every day, even when our circumstances are ordinary or even difficult. His love is so full, and his grace so boundless, that when his Spirit lives in us even a flat tire can feel like a blessing. Our status as beloved daughters of the King guarantees it, we need only claim it.

God, I am yours. You have given me grace in abundance, and I am so thankful.

DAY 94

REBUILDING

The LORD will rebuild Jerusalem;
there his glory will be seen.
PSALM 102:16 NCV

You will have a lot of thoughts about your day ahead—grocery lists, medical appointments, sports training, or where you put those keys! We are so consumed with our thoughts of all of the details of the day ahead that we forget to think on the greatness of God.

When we allow our thoughts of God to take over, we see our small concerns about the day fall away. Ask God to break through your stresses and help you concentrate on what matters the most today. Thank him that in the times of deepest need he is the water of life you can draw your strength from.

Father, I need to drink deeply from your well of life today. Thank you for the strength that is abundant in you.

God will not move you into something without giving you the grace to make it through.

DAY 95

Changing Seasons

He made the moon to mark the seasons;
the sun knows its time for setting.
Psalm 104:19 ESV

You will, undoubtedly, have various seasons in your life: seasons of longing and contentment, seasons of discouragement and joy, seasons of more and less. Being a grown-up means stretching into new ways of living, and this usually doesn't happen until the season hits.

Don't make excuses for why you can't do what God is calling you to do. Be brave! God will not move you into something without giving you the grace you need to make it through. The Lord has placed a calling on your life, and he will give you the courage to know that he is with you when he calls you to step forward.

God, in all the seasons of life, you have been faithful to me. Show me what is next in your plan.

DAY 96

THINGS UNKNOWN

"Call to Me, and I will answer you, and show you great and mighty things, which you do not know.'"

JEREMIAH 33:3 NKJV

"If you're there God, give me a sign!" People have screamed this into the heavens many times throughout the years. We want to see something that will tell us that God is real—and not just real, but also present. We want that experience that will bring heaven to earth and expel our doubt with a single lightning bolt. But he is so much more than experience.

We mistakenly think experience is the peak of his power. Other gods can perform miracles and deliver experiences, but the one true God continues to show his power in the valley. He is even in the valley of the shadow of death where miracles seem non-existent. Those other gods have nothing to offer us in despair. God will show us great and mighty things. He is not limited by time, space, or human understanding.

God, I put my hope and faith in you for things that are unknown. You are not surprised by anything.

DAY 97

Words Matter

Do not let any unwholesome talk come out of your mouths, but only what is helpful for building others up according to their needs, that it may benefit those who listen.

EPHESIANS 4:29 NIV

"Sticks and stones will break my bones, but words will never harm me." This often-quoted childhood rhyme isn't true at all. Words do hurt. They matter. Taunts, rants, and criticisms hurt the hearers, and God has called us to build up one another. How you speak with others will define you. Do your friends consider you trustworthy or incapable of keeping a secret? Are you a gossip? Do you use your words as a weapon, or are your conversations encouraging and helpful?

Keeping our conversations wholesome and heartwarming can be gratifying for both speakers and hearers. Choose your words and conversations carefully. Take a moment to gather your thoughts before speaking and especially before responding. Don't return one mean statement with another. Being kind in thought, word, and deed are qualities to aim for.

Father, give me patience to speak kindly to others. I want to use my words to bless and encourage.

DAY 98

LISTENING TO GOD

After the earthquake came a fire, but the LORD was not in the fire. And after the fire came a gentle whisper.

1 KINGS 19:12 NIV

A surprising study on parenting styles revealed that one of the best ways to get the attention of a child is to whisper. When instructing an important lesson, imparting it in a whisper helps the child to focus, to remember, and to act upon the information. Yelling doesn't work as well. Taking the child onto your lap or sitting closely and softly speaking causes both memory and comprehension to improve. This is true with your heavenly Father. He wants to share so very much with you.

God longs to tell you of his unfathomable love for you. He wants to lighten your burdens and help you grow. Are you willing to listen to his still, small voice? Let him whisper in your ear. Take a deep breath, sink back into his arms, and allow him to feed your soul.

Father, help me to listen quietly to you today. You have so much to tell me.

DAY 99

Confident Trust

Do not throw away this confident trust in the Lord. Remember the great reward it brings you!

HEBREWS 10:35 NLT

After an entire book dedicated to validating and strengthening a Christian's confidence in Christ, this warning is issued: do not lose it. Maintain your confidence and trust in God. In the end, it will be rewarded.

The best way to remain confident is by remembering the truths of the Gospel. We must immerse ourselves regularly in the Word so the subtle lies and twisting of truth that the world constantly bombards us with do not begin to corrupt our confidence. Hold fast to the Father and ask for wisdom to discern truth from the lies. Confidently stand on faith in him alone. He is the only way.

God, I want to surround myself with your truth. Show me the best way to do this.

DAY 100

Power

"You will receive power when the Holy Spirit comes on you."

Acts 1:8 NIV

After Jesus's ascension, he gave the promised gift of the Holy Spirit to the disciples. They were told to wait for this gift before they proceeded any further. Jesus knew it would be fruitless to attempt to carry out any exploits unless his followers were filled with his Spirit. As they waited, the Holy Spirit came and filled them with power. This was a power they lacked prior to this moment. It wasn't something they could conjure up on their own. Jesus wanted them to know that a new power would come.

That same power is there for all of us who ask. God hasn't given us a spirit of fear but one of power. You don't need your own power, God will give you his through the Holy Spirit.

God, thank you for the gift of your Spirit. I lean on him today for the power to live like you want me to.